October

Julie Murray

Abdo
MONTHS
Kids

abdopublishing.com

Published by Abdo Kids, a division of ABDO, PO Box 398166, Minneapolis, Minnesota 55439.
Copyright © 2018 by Abdo Consulting Group, Inc. International copyrights reserved in all countries.
No part of this book may be reproduced in any form without written permission from the publisher.

Printed in the United States of America, North Mankato, Minnesota.

052017

092017

THIS BOOK CONTAINS
RECYCLED MATERIALS

Photo Credits: Getty Images, iStock, Library of Congress, Shutterstock

Production Contributors: Teddy Borth, Jennie Forsberg, Grace Hansen

Design Contributors: Christina Doffing, Candice Keimig, Dorothy Toth

Publisher's Cataloging in Publication Data

Names: Murray, Julie, 1969-, author.

Title: October / by Julie Murray.

Description: Minneapolis, Minnesota : Abdo Kids, 2018 | Series: Months |
    Includes bibliographical references and index.

Identifiers: LCCN 2016962343 | ISBN 9781532100246 (lib. bdg.) |
    ISBN 9781532100932 (ebook) | ISBN 9781532101489 (Read-to-me ebook)

Subjects: LCSH: October (Month)--Juvenile literature. | Calendar--Juvenile literature.

Classification: DDC 398/.33--dc23

LC record available at http://lccn.loc.gov/2016962343

Table of Contents

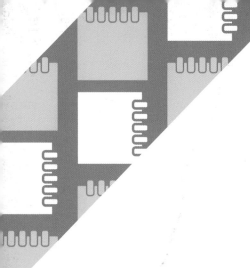

October

There are 12 months in the year.

January

February

March

April

May

June

July

August

September

October

November

December

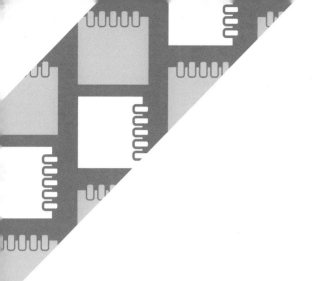

October is the 10th month.

It has 31 days.

October

1	2	3	4	5	6	7
8	9	10	11	12	13	14
15	16	17	18	19	20	21
22	23	24	25	26	27	28
29	30	31				

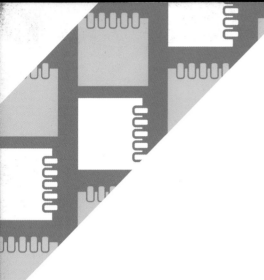

Eleanor Roosevelt was born in October. Her birthday is on the 11th.

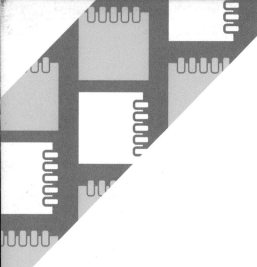

Diwali is sometimes in October.

Priya celebrates with her family.

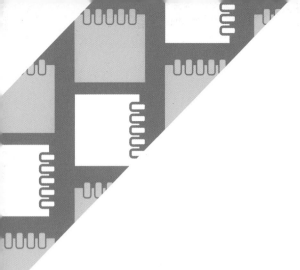

Trick or Treat? It's Halloween!

It is on the 31st.

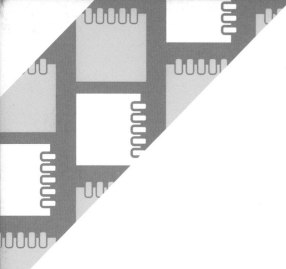

The days get colder in October.

Jess wears a hat.

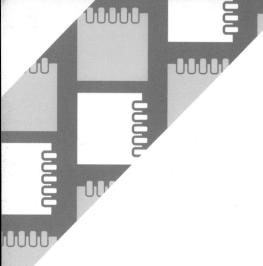

The trees turn pretty colors.

Emma finds a red leaf.

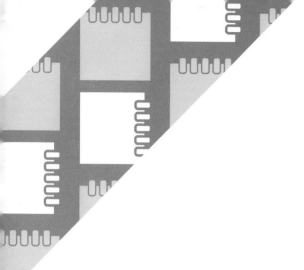

Leaves fall from trees.

Katy rakes leaves.

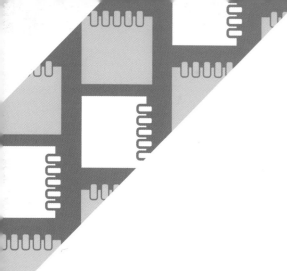

Greg picks a pumpkin.

He loves October!

Fun Days in October

World Animal Day
October 4

World Teachers' Day
October 5

Global Handwashing Day
October 15

National Cat Day
October 29

Glossary

Diwali
a religious Hindu festival that celebrates good winning over evil, and honors the goddess Lakshmi.

Eleanor Roosevelt
the First Lady of the United States (1933-1945) who was very active in American politics and equal rights.

Index

abdokids.com

Use this code to log on to abdokids.com and access crafts, games, videos, and more!

Abdo Kids Code:
MOK0246